My First FIVE TASTES of Tibetan Buddhism

a poetry cycle
in seven languages

Manuel N. Gómez

AuthorHouse™
1663 Liberty Drive
Bloomington, IN 47403
www.authorhouse.com
Phone: 1 (833) 262-8899

This book is printed on acid-free paper.

ISBN: 978-1-6655-0037-1(sc)
ISBN: 978-1-6655-0036-4 (e)

Library of Congress Control Number: 2020917934

Print information available on the last page.

Published by AuthorHouse 09/22/2020

“Three things cannot be

long hidden:

the sun, the moon,

and the truth.”

~ The Buddha

My First
FIVE TASTES

of Tibetan Buddhism

Manuel N. Gómez

For
Maya & Tomás

CONTENTS

INTRODUCTION

In my life there are certain memories I hold close to me. High among them are my experiences in India. It was in 2010 that I was invited to join a group of students from UC Irvine on a two week journey to India. My wife and I eagerly accepted. The itinerary included one week visiting Dharamasala, and attending The Dalai Lama's annual lectures on the Heart Sutra. We also were given an opportunity to visit and dialogue with students enrolled in the Tibetan Children's Village and Sarah College for Higher Tibetan Studies. The memories of our travels, our new friends, and our adventures have not been forgotten. In Delhi, Tibetan Buddhist monks graciously invited us into their home. In Dharamasala we were pleased to have an audience with His Holiness the Dalai Lama. In Mundgod we had a memorable week delightfully mesmerized in the joys of living inside the daily rhythms and routines of a working Tibetan monastery.

It is April 2004 and His Holiness the XIV Dalai Lama is sitting on a chair on the stage of the Bren Events Center at the University of California, Irvine. He is participating in a program entitled "Ethical Leadership Through Compassion: A Dialogue Between Youth Leaders and The Dalai Lama." Prior to speaking, HHDL begins by formally receiving California high school student delegations bringing gifts that reflect projects they carried out in their respective communities the

2010 UCI delegation with HH Dalai Lama, Dharamsala, India ~ Back row, from left: Julio Benitez, Alex Wong, Kevin Truong, Vienna Nguyen, Bethel Mesgana, His Holiness the XIV Dalai Lama, Jasmine Fang, Herb Killackey, Manuel Gomez, Leslie Millerd Rogers. Front row: Karina Hamilton, Genet Gomez, Bibi Do, Jennifer Linh Phan, Mani Dhaliwal, Vivien Phung, Duyet Do

prior semester. For example, the The Dalai Lama received an informative video documenting a mural project, a photo album showing the work of students giving food and blankets to the homeless, and other similar tokens of appreciation. As the project documents were received, the students were thanked and the gifts were routinely placed in a box by an assistant. However, one notable exception occurred with a gift of a simple pair of working gloves that reflected the projects students had completed cleaning up littered streets and doing some gardening. When HHDL saw the gloves he held them up for the audience to see and joyfully said "Oh, I can use these!" He then carefully placed them inside a personal small carrying bag.

This simple act revealed an awareness — for us to see — to free ourselves, we ourselves must be willing to do the hard work.

Another story I will share occurred when we attended The Dalai Lama's Heart Sutra lectures in Dharamasala.

On the third day of the lectures, he talked about the Buddhist concept of "Emptiness" or "Selflessness", which are, as he indicated, with a sly smile, not easy concepts to grasp. Our group was fortunate to be granted a private audience with HHDL. On the morning our meeting was scheduled, I awoke to the discovery that there was absolutely no water coming from the hotel faucets or shower. I turned the faucet and found nothing but emptiness.

During our audience, I shared my morning experience with HHDL, indicating that it had helped me to grasp the meaning of Emptiness. I told my story of turning the faucet and seeing emptiness, no water, not a single drop. The result was the same with the shower, emptiness. HHDL suddenly places his hand on my forehead and briskly pushes on my head declaring, "You are not talking about Emptiness! You are talking about nothingness!" He then laughs jovially and we all laugh with him. I am left with the knowledge that while I may know something about "nothingness," I still do not understand "emptiness".

I do know our world is in a time of turmoil. We are experiencing a difficult and dangerous turn. Social systems are in deep crisis. We are all in pain and from our divided spaces we rage against ourselves and each other. We live in a land where people no longer know the difference between the truth and a lie, fact or fiction, real or fake. We are becoming strangers to each other. Our present moment foretells of prolonged social struggles for human dignity and enduring resistance to tyranny. With growing social inequality, increasing intolerance, and numbing political and environmental cruelty, our world is in desperate need of seekers of justice and truth. HHDL is one of these seekers I most admire. He embodies ethical and compassionate leadership in a world where we are all in need of a little more compassion.

Poetry has the creative power to raise our expectations and awaken our minds to see the world anew, even if for just one brief revelatory moment. The creative arts can help make our differences become less significant, allowing us to focus our attention in the universal reality of our common human bond. Beyond all the border lines and walls of separation, poetry liberates the human imagination. Indeed, this is why I have asked friends to translate these poems to their home languages. It is my hope that this effort will reach far more people than is possible with a monolingual book.

The five poems in this book were written soon after my return from India. Simply put — they are my first five tastes of Tibetan Buddhism.

~ Manuel N. Gómez, Ph.D.

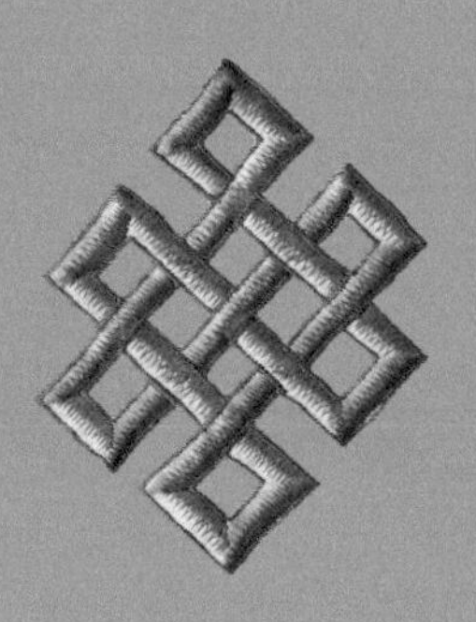

KARMIC FRUIT: First Taste

Hurt others
Hurt yourself

Help others
Help yourself

Speak harsh words
Hungry ghosts will visit you

Speak soft words
Happiness awaits you

Think negative thoughts
Hell will visit you

Think positive thoughts
Sweet karma awaits you

SUFFERING: Second Taste

Into this world
We are born
Whoever or whatever
Comes together
Will be torn apart

We are all
Each and everyone
Caught inside
The jaws of Time

Whatever we do
Whatever we build
Will not last
All will fall

Time's dark shadow
We can be sure
Awaits us all

IGNORANCE: Third Taste

Not knowing why
Open your eyes
See the suffering
Not knowing why
See the blindness

Not knowing why
Open your eyes
See the dreams

Not knowing why
See the sadness

Not knowing why
Open your eyes
See the lies

Not knowing why
See the madness

Now knowing why
Open your eyes

See the root cause
Now knowing why
See happiness

It is possible
Open your eyes

It is possible
To see the reason why
Wisdom is emptiness

COMPASSION: Fourth Taste

With a kind heart
Hold all others
More dear than self
Bring no harm to others

With true peace of mind
Practice patience
Let your enemies
Become your teachers

With loving kindness
Carry the burden for
The benefit of others
Bring all blame upon yourself

Everything we do
Think or say
Every action we take
Comes back to us
One day

Let your mind see
We are all one ocean
One universe, one family
Dependent on each other
In love and compassion

ENLIGHTENMENT: Fifth Taste

Let go of the past
Let go of the self
You are not helpless
You are your only protector

We have but a brief time here
Calm your consciousness
Abandon anger, fear, and desire
Pleasure or pain
It is all the same

The door is open

~ Manuel N. Gómez

FRUTA DEL KARMA: Primer Sentido

Lastimando a otros
Te lastimas tú mismo

Ayudando a otros
Te ayudas tú mismo

Platicando palabras desagradables
El espanto hambriento te va a visitar

Platicando palabras suaves
La felicidad te espera

Pensando pensamientos negativos
El infierno te va a visitar

Pensando pensamientos positivos
Dulce Karma te espera

SUFRIMIENTO: Segundo Sentido

En este mundo
Nacimos
Cada uno
Atrapado dentro de
Las mandíbulas del Tiempo

Cualquier cosa qué hacemos
Cualquier cosa qué construimos
No durara
Todo se caerá

La sombra oscura seguros
Nos espera a todos

IGNORANCIA: Tercer Sentido

Sin saber por qué
Habré tus ojos
Ve el sufrimiento

Sin saber por qué
Ve la ceguera

Sin saber por qué
Habré tus ojos
Ve los suenos
Sin saber por qué
Ve la tristeza

Sin saber por qué
Habré tus ojos
Ve las mentiras
Sin saber por qué
Ve la locura

Ahora sabiendo por qué
Habré tus ojos
Ve la raiz de la causa
Ahora sabiendo por qué
Ve felicidad

Es posible
Habré tus ojos
Es posible
Ver la razón por la cual
El vació es sabiduría

COMPASIÓN: Cuarto Sentido

Con Corazón cariñoso
Estima mas a los demás
Qué a ti mismo
No le hagas daño a nadie

Con verdadera tranquilidad de espíritu
Practica paciencia
Qué sean tus enemigos
Tus maestros

Con tierno cariño
Lleva la carga
En beneficio de los demás
Lleva toda la culpa tú mismo

Todo lo qué hacemos
Pensamos o decimos
Cada acción qué tomamos
Nos regresa
Algún dia

Deja qué tú mente miré

Somos todos un mar

Una familia grande

Dependiendo unos de los otros

En amor y compación

ILUMINACIÓN: Quinto Sentido

Olvida el pasado
Olvidate tú mismo
No eres incapaz
Eres tú único protector

Tenemos solo breve tiempo aquí
Calma tú conciencia
Abandona el coraje, el miedo,
Y el deseo
Placer o dolor
Es todo lo mismo

La puerta esta abierta

~ Manuel N. Gómez
Spanish translation by Nydia Hernandez

五つの味

業の果物 ー 第一の味

人を傷つけると、
自分が傷つく

人を助けると、
自分が救われる

険しい言葉は
餓鬼をよびよせ

柔らかい言葉は
喜びを招く

否定は
地獄につながり

肯定は
運命を切り開く

苦悩 — 第二の味

この世界に、私たちは生まれ
誰一人として
時間の歯車から逃れられない

人が何をしようと
何を作ろうと
すべては無に帰す

時間の暗い影のみが
私たちに与えられた真実なのだ。

無知　－　第三の味

理(ことわり)を知らずに目を開ければ
見えるものは苦悩
なぜかはわからず
暗黒の世界を見る

理を知らずに目を開ければ、
見えるものは蜃気楼
わからないままに
悲しみを見る

なぜかを知らずに目を開ければ、
見えるものは嘘
わからない目に
見えるものは混沌

理を知り
目を開ければ、
見えてくるのはすべての源
なぜかがわかれば
喜びが見える

目を開け！
知とは空なのだから

共感　–　第四の味

親切な心は、
自分よりも人を大切にする
誰をも傷つけない

真の平安を心に持って、
耐え、敵から学ぼうとする

愛と優しさで、
他人の重荷を背負い、
謗りを一身に引き受ける

すべてはいつか自分に帰ってくる
どの行いも——。
どの言葉も——。

見えるだろうか
私たちはみんな一つの海、一つの家族、
お互いに頼りあって生きている
愛と共感の中で

悟り　–　第五の味

過去にとらわれず、
自分にとらわれず、
君は無力ではないのだから
君は自分の守護神だ

この世で過ごすのはほんの一瞬
意識を鎮め
怒りも恐れも欲望も、すべて捨て去れ

快楽も痛みも
所詮は同じ

君の前に、今、扉は開いている

~ Manuel N. Gómez
Japanese translation by Ryuko Flores

NHÂN QUẢ NGHIỆP: Vị Thứ Nhất

Làm tổn thương kẻ khác
Là làm đau chính mình

Giúp đỡ người chung quanh
Là cứu giúp chính mình

Nói lên lời cay độc
Quỷ ma khát máu tìm

Nói những lời dịu êm
Hạnh phúc luôn chào đón

Nuôi tư tưởng đen tối
Địa ngục đang chực chờ

Nghĩ những điều tốt đẹp
Nghiệp lành đợi đâu đây

ĐAU KHỔ: Vị Thứ Hai

Chúng ta sinh ra
Trong thế giới này
Bất cứ điều gì, bất cứ ai
Kết hợp lại
Rồi cũng chia phôi

Tất cả chúng ta
Không chừa một ai
Đều bị vướng chặt
Giữa đôi hàm thời gian

Bất luận ta làm chi
Hay đắp xây điều gì
Không bao giờ tồn tại
Thảy đều sẽ tan đi

Bóng tối của thời gian
Chúng ta biết chắc
Đang chờ đợi mỗi người

U MÊ: Vị Thứ Ba

Nếu không hiểu vì sao
Hãy mở mắt ra
Để tỏ tường giấc mộng
Nếu không hiểu vì sao
Hãy nhìn rõ nỗi buồn

Nếu không hiểu vì sao
Hãy mở mắt ra
Để thấy điều gian dối
Nếu không hiểu vì sao
Hãy trông nỗi điên cuồng

Nếu không hiểu vì sao
Hãy mở mắt ra
Để thấy rõ nguồn cơn
Nếu không hiểu vì sao
Hãy ngắm nhìn hạnh phúc

Thật là dễ dàng
Khi mở mắt ra
Thật là dễ dàng
Khi hiểu vì sao
Trí tuệ chỉ là trống rỗng

LÒNG TRẮC ẨN: Vị Thứ Tư

Với trái tim nhân ái
Hãy ôm lấy mọi người
Thân yêu hơn bản ngã
Đừng làm ai khổ đau

Với bình yên trong tâm
Hãy tập lòng nhẫn nại
Hãy để cho kẻ thù
Thành người thầy của ta
Với lòng tử tế
Hãy vác gánh nặng
Giùm mọi người
Và cam nhận mọi phiền trách

Những gì chúng ta làm
Suy nghĩ hay nói ra
Hành động của chúng ta
Một ngày không xa
Sẽ quay trở lại

Hãy cho tâm ta thấy được
Mỗi người là một đại dương
Một vũ trụ, một gia đình
Thảy đều nương tựa vào nhau
Trong thương yêu và trắc ẩn

IAI NGỘ: Vị Thứ Năm

Hãy buông thả quá khứ
Hãy buông thả bản thân
Bạn không cô đơn
Bạn là người bảo vệ lấy mình

Ta chỉ có một thời ở chốn này
Hãy trấn an tâm thức
Từ bỏ sân hận, sợ hãi, ham muốn
Khoái lạc hay khổ đau
Tất cả đều giống nhau

Cửa đã mở

~ Manuel N. Gómez
Vietnamese translation by Tri C. Tran

REFLECTIONS
OF THE
JOURNEY
in photographs

Sitting with young monastic students, Mundgod, India

Students gathering for UCI welcome presentation

PHOTO BY LESLIE MILLERD ROGERS

Greeting HH XIV Dalai Lama, UC Irvine (2015)

Architectural pillar at the Library of Tibetan Works and Archives, Dharamsala, India

Showing HH XIV Dalai Lama UCI / Bowers Museum publication
Tibet: Treasures from the Roof of the World *(2011)*

Prayer Hill, Mundgod, India

Tibetan Children's Village welcomes UCI visitors (2010)

Mural in Sarah College, Dharamsala, India

Young monastic students entering debate hall at Gaden Shartse Monastery

Daily sweeping the Monastery grounds, Mundgod, India

카르마 열매: 첫 번째 입맛

타인을 해하라
네 자신을 해하라

타인을 도와라
네 자신을 도와라

냉혹한 말을 뱉어라
배고픈 악귀들이 찾아올 것이다

부드러운 말을 건네라
행복이 기다릴 것이다

부정적인 생각을 하여라
지옥이 찾아올 것이다

긍정적인 생각을 하여라
달콤한 카르마가 기다릴 것이다

고통: 두 번째 입맛

이 세상 속
우리는 태어난다
그 누구던 그 무엇이던
섞여흐르다가 곧
흩어질 것이다

우리는 다
각자 모두가
시간의 흐름에
빠져있다

우리가 무엇을 하던
우리가 무엇을 쌓던
영원하지 않으며
무너질 것이다

시간의 검은 그림자는
확실히
우리 모두를 기다린다

무지: 세 번째 입맛

이유를 모른 채
눈을 뜨고
고통을 보아라
이유를 모른 채
가려진 것을 보아라

이유를 모른 채
눈을 뜨고
꿈을 보아라
이유를 모른 채
슬픔을 보아라

이유를 모른 채
눈을 뜨고
거짓을 보아라
이유를 모른 채
화를 보아라

이제는 이유를 알고
눈을 떠라
본질적 이유를 보아라
이제는 이유를 알고
행복을 보아라

눈을 뜨는 건
가능하다
이유를 보는 건
가능하다

긍휼: 네 번째 입맛

따뜻한 마음으로
다른 이들을 어루만져 주어라
나 보다는 남들을
남들에게 해를 끼치지 말아라

진정한 평화로
인내를 훈련하라
네 적을
네 선생이 되게 하라

애정 어린 선한 마음으로
다른이들을 위해
짐을 짊어지어라
모든 책임을 지어라

우리가 하는
모든 생각, 모든 말
모든 행동은
언젠가
우리에게 돌아 온다

네 마음이 보게 하라
우리는 하나의 바다이다
하나의 세상, 하나의 가족
사랑과 긍휼함으로
서로에게 기대어 있다

깨우침: 다섯번째 입맛

과거를 보내어라
네 자신을 보내어라
너는 무력하지 않으며
네 자신의 유일한 보호막이다

우리는 짧은 시간동안 이 곳에 있다
생각을 진정시켜라
화, 두려움,
욕망을 버려라
기쁨과 고통
이는 곧 같다

그 문은 열려 있다

마누엘 고메즈
~ Manuel N. Gómez
Korean translation by Erika Yun

業報水果：前味

傷害別人
傷了自己

幫助別人
幫助自己

說難聽的話
餓鬼來找你

說溫柔話語
快樂等待你

想負面的想法
地獄將拜訪你

思想正面的想法
甜美果報等著你

痛苦：第二味

來到這個世界
我們初生
不論誰或不論如何
走到一起
將被撕裂分離

我們都是
一個人　；每個人
卡住在
時間的齒輪內

無論我們做什麼
無論我們建設什麼
都不會持續
所有將塌下

時間的黑影
我們可以肯定的
等待著所有的我們

無知：第三味

不知道為什麼
睜開你的眼睛
看到苦難
不知道為什麼
看見失明

不知道為什麼
睜開你的眼睛
看見夢想

不知道為什麼
看到悲傷

不知道為什麼
睜開你的眼睛
看到謊言

不知道為什麼
看到瘋狂

現在知道為什麼
睜開你的眼睛
看見根源

現在知道為什麼
看見幸福

有可能的
睜開你的眼睛

有可能的
看見原因 為什麼
智慧是空

同情：第四味

以一顆好心
保持所有其他的
比自我更親愛
不帶來傷害他人

隨著心靈的真正的和平
學會忍耐
讓你的敵人
成為你的老師

隨著慈愛
攜帶負擔
為他人的利益
將所有的指責給自己

我們所做的一切
想的或是說的
我們採取每一個行動
都回給自己
有一天

讓你的心看到
我們都是一個海洋
一個宇宙，一個家族
依賴對方
在愛和同情心裏

啟蒙照耀：第五味

放手過去
放開自我
你不是束手無策
你是你唯一的保護

我們有，但一個當下短暫的時間
平靜你的意識
放棄憤怒，恐懼，和慾望
快樂或痛苦
這都是一樣的

門是開著的

~ Manuel N. Gómez
Chinese translation by Jasmine Fang

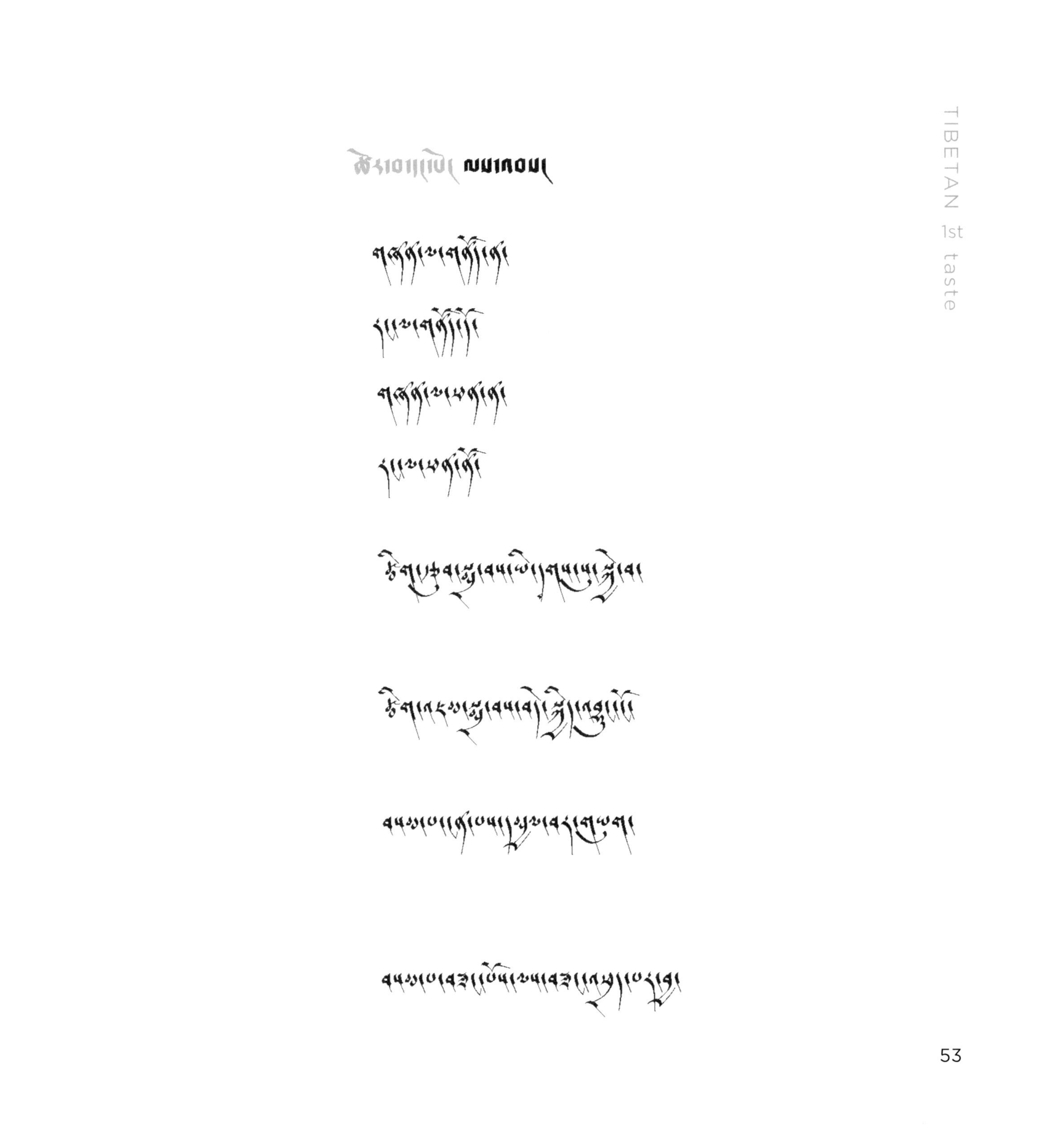

[illegible]

[illegible]

[illegible]

[illegible]

[illegible]

[illegible]

[illegible]

[illegible]

[illegible]

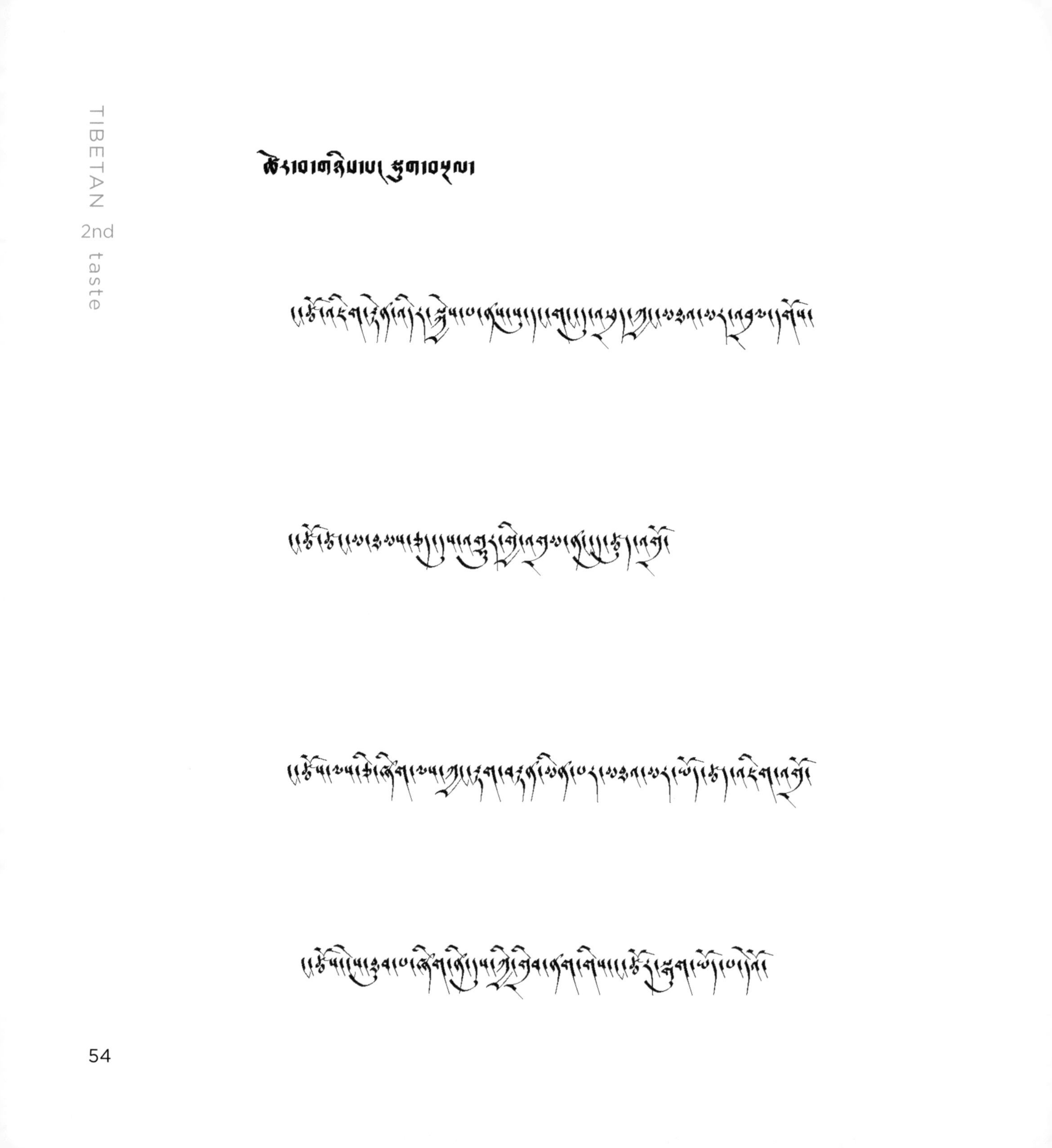

TIBETAN 2nd taste

ཚིར་བ་གཉིས་པ། རྒྱག་བཙལ།

[illegible]

[illegible]

[illegible]

[illegible]

ཚོར་བ་གསུམ་པ། ཉིན་ལེ་ཁ།

མིག་ལ་ཞེན་ཀྱི།། ཡ་རྒྱ་ག་ཞལ་ཟས་མཆོ།། ཁོ་ན་རྒྱུ་མཚན་ག་ས་ཡ་བར།

ཚོ་ཡ་བ་རྒྱུར་ཁོ་ན་རྒྱུ་མཚན་ག་ས་ཡ་བར།

མིག་ལ་ཞེན་ཀྱི།། ཡ་སྐྱ་ལ་ས་མཆོ།། ཁོ་ན་རྒྱུ་མཚན་ག་ས་ཡ་བར།

རྩོ་ཞ་ས་མཆོ།། ཁོ་ན་རྒྱུ་མཚན་ག་ས་ཡ་བར།

མིག་ལ་ཞེན་ཀྱི།། ཡ་རྡུག་ས་མཆོ།། ཁོ་ན་རྒྱུ་མཚན་ག་ས་ཡ་བར།

སྡུག་བ་མཆོ།། ཁོ་ན་རྒྱུ་མཚན་ག་ས་ཡ་བར།

མིག་ལ་ཞེན་ཀྱི།། ཡ་སྐྱུ་རྩུག་མཆོ།། ཁོ་ན་རྒྱུ་མཚན་གི་ཡ་རྒྱུར་ཤིས།

།།གཟེ།།ཞེ།།ཞ་མཛེ།།ཁ་ཏེ་རྒྱ་མཚན་ཀེ།།ཡ་ཁ་རྒྱུར།

།།ཀྱེ་ཡེ།།ཁ་ཞིག་ཟེ།

ཀྱི་ཀྱི་ཡིག་ཙ་སྐྱེས།།

ཤ་ཡ་ར་བ་ཀེ་ཟེ།།ཁ་ཀྱེ།།ཡེ་ཀ་ཁ་ཏེ་རྒྱ་མཚན་ཀ་ཤ་ཡ་ཀྱེ།།ཁ་ཞིག་ཟེ།།

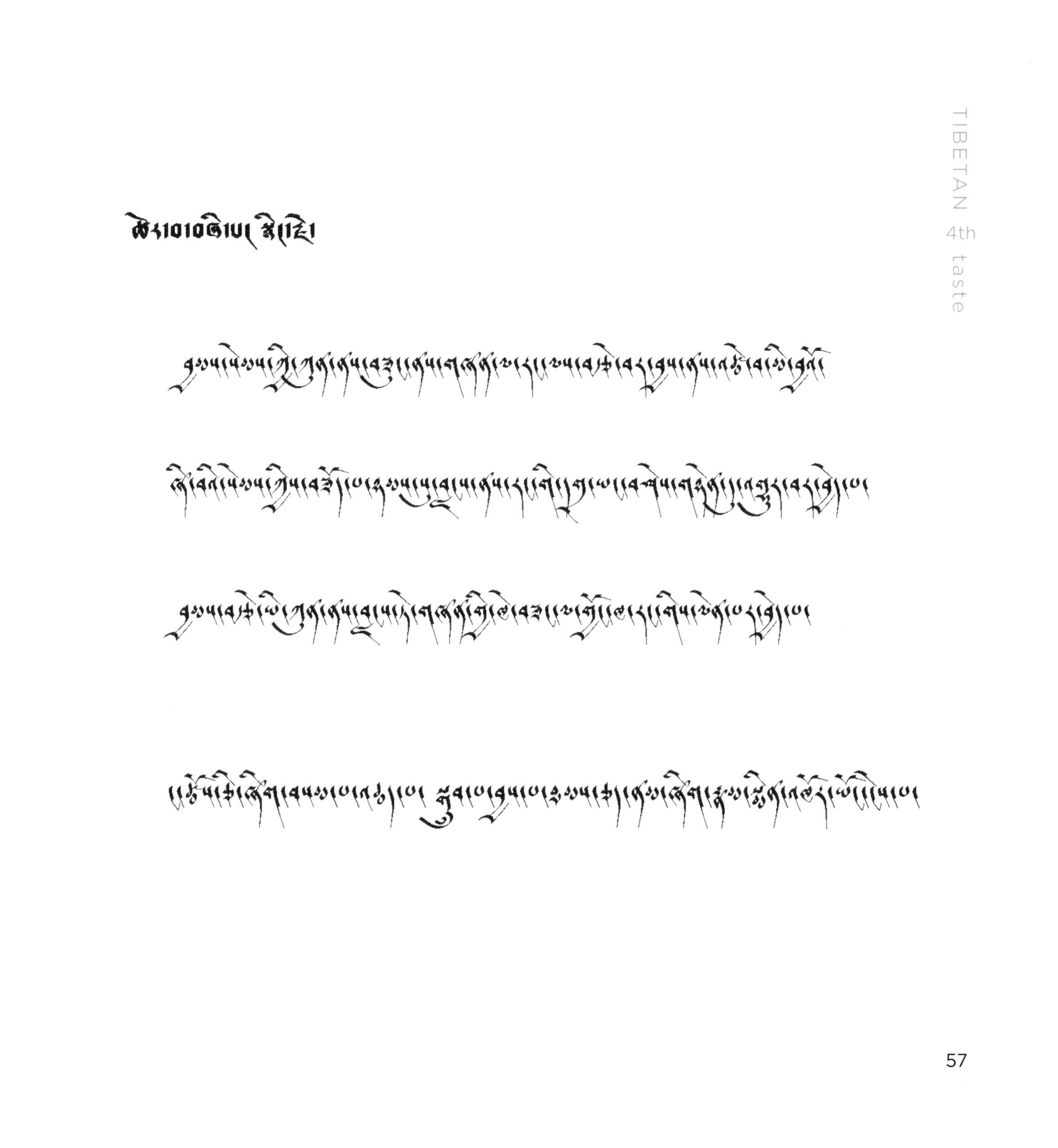

[illegible]

[illegible]

[illegible]

[illegible]

[illegible]

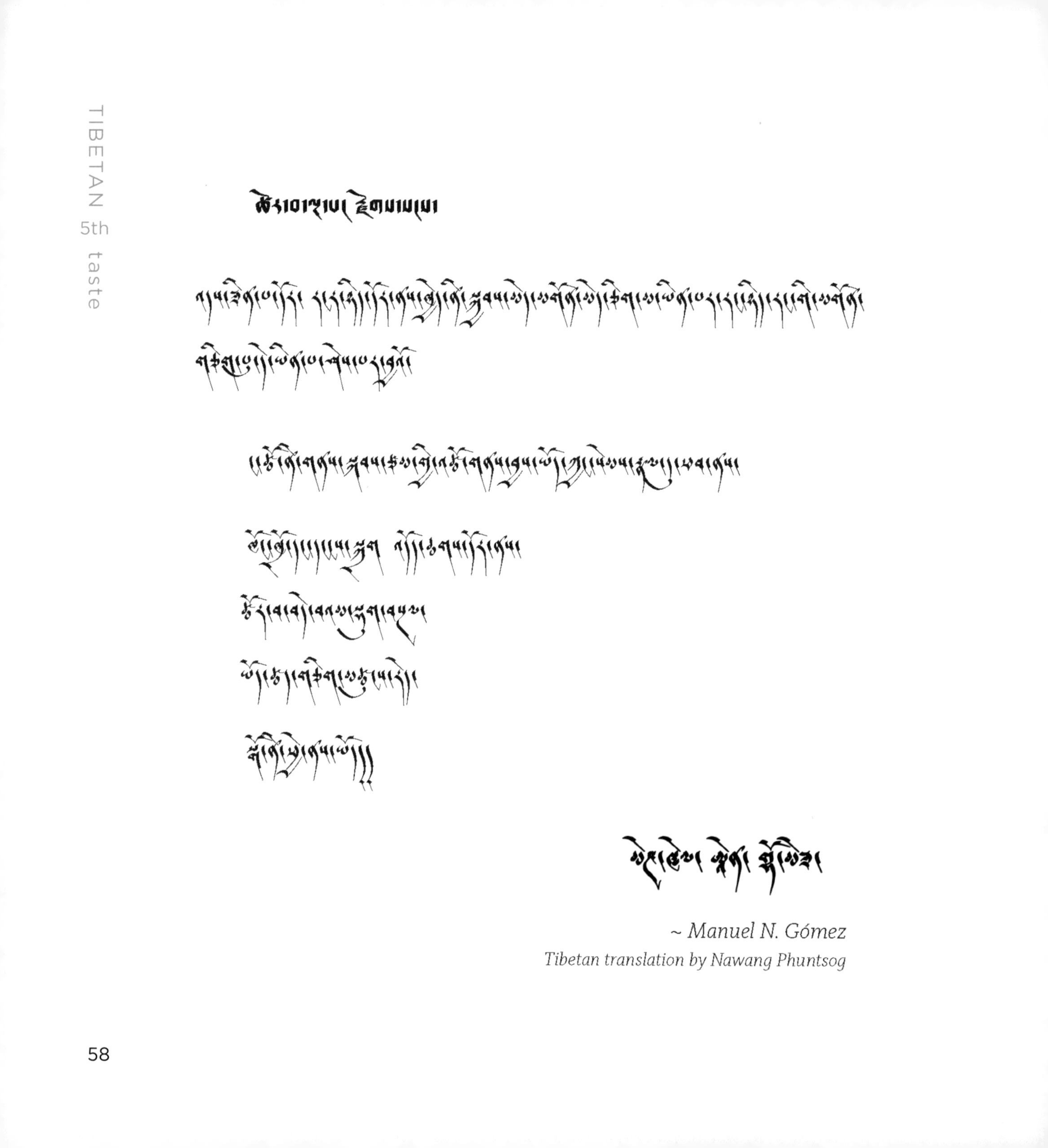

[illegible]

[illegible]

[illegible]

[illegible]

[illegible]

[illegible]

[illegible]

[illegible]

[illegible]

~ Manuel N. Gómez

Tibetan translation by Nawang Phuntsog

ACKNOWLEDGEMENTS

I am grateful to so many friends, and feel indebted to wonderful colleagues. There are many individuals I must acknowledge for their support. First and foremost, I need to give deep thanks to Cynthia Love, Creative Director and my anchor for actually getting this book designed and published. Cindy, I can never thank you enough for all your vital assistance. I want to convey my heartfelt appreciation to Johanna Love for the wonderful photographs she took for this book. I thank my brother-in-law Stephen Cadena for his help during a thorny moment in my writing, and thanks also to Hye-Won Shin for her assistance with a referral.

I am exceedingly grateful to each one of my colleagues and friends who willingly gave of their time, knowledge, and insight to provide the various translations of my five poems from the English language to their respective languages in Spanish, Japanese, Korean, Vietnamese, Chinese, and Tibetan. They are: Nydia Figueroa Hernandez, Jasmine I. Fang, Ryuko Flores, Tri C. Tran, Erica Yun, and Nawang Phunstog.

I also want to convey my appreciation to the Office of His Holiness the XIV Dalai Lama, Gashar Khenpo Rinpoche, Jangchup Choeden, and the gracious monks at Gaden Shartse Norling Monastery. Kalon Tempa Tsering and his staff at

Delhi Bureau of His Holiness the Dalai Lama and Kunsang Dorjee, Deputy Secretary and Protocol Officer, Department of Information and International Relations, Central Tibetan Administration, and Geshe Tenzin Dawa and the wonderful staff at Namgyal Kyi Tsel Guest House. All have my enduring gratitude.

Bibi Do, staff member in the History Department of UC Irvine and Duyet Do deserve special mention. It was Bibi who, on behalf of the students, invited us on this trip. Duyet was the principle organizer of all the logistics for this complex journey. The experience was made so much more memorable because of the wonderful UCI students who so actively participated in this extraordinary international exchange with Tibetan culture and monastic education. I would be neglectful not mentioning Karina Hamilton, Herb P. Killacky, and Leslie Millerd, UCI colleagues who also joined in support of the students on this trip to India.

My daughter Maya and my son Tomas, always eager to join our adventurous travels were atypically unable to come with us due to their own busy lives. I am always stimulated by our conversations and your intelligent sometimes surprising and unexpected perspectives. To my wife Genet, whom I rely on way too much to be my memory, thank you for all you do and most of all, for joining me on this unforgettable journey.

~ Manuel N. Gómez

January 2020

MANUEL GÓMEZ was born in Santa Ana, California. He served as Vice Chancellor for Student Affairs at the University of California, Irvine, and is nationally recognized for his leadership in creating and managing educational programs to obtain greater access for vulnerable populations; he helped propel UCI's diversity and excellence to the top ranks of universities in the world.

He is also recognized leader in Free Speech issues and academic freedom, diversity struggles, research publications for the advancement of learning, and establishment of international exchange programs. He is the Founder of the Dalai Lama Scholars Program. He is the recipient of the UC Irvine Medal, the highest honor UCI confers on extraordinary individuals who have contributed significantly to the success of the University. He is also a published poet. His recent book is entitled: *Dancing With The Sun: The Artwork of Manuel Hernandez Trujillo.*

Photo by Genet Chavez Gómez

"No one saves us but ourselves,

no one can and no one may,

we ourselves

must walk the path."

~ The Buddha

Printed in the United States
By Bookmasters